CW00406741

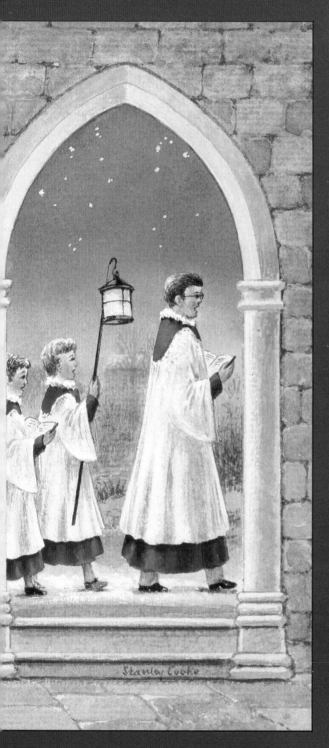

Processional carol singing by church choirs became popular after the 'Festival of Nine Lessons and Carols' was introduced at Truro Cathedral in the late 1880s.

Carols

While it's hard to craft an exact definition for the word 'carol', *The Oxford Companion To Music* gives one of the most accurate descriptions: 'A religious seasonal song, of joyful character, in the vernacular and sung by the common people.'

Carols are the epitome of popular music – unlike hymns (specifically written to praise God), their roots lie in simple folk songs that were sung in the open air on pagan feast days. After Christianity came to Britain's shores in the early Middle Ages, carols were gradually absorbed into the Church, especially after it adopted and renamed certain pagan festivals for its own calendar. But carols fared badly under the Puritans, who banned their singing (and any celebration of Christmas) for a decade or so in the 17th century.

Music scholars say we owe our greatest thanks to the Victorians – who reinvented various Christmas traditions – for the survival of some of our oldest and loveliest carols. Whatever the debate, most of us would agree ... Christmas simply isn't Christmas without any carols!

In the beginning...

The earliest known carols involved dancing as well as singing and the word 'carol' itself is thought to be derived from the French word 'caroler', the Latin 'choraula', the Greek 'choraules' before that, and ultimately 'choros'. The 'choros' was a circle dance that was part of wider religious celebrations and fertility rites.

Pagan popularity

Before Christianity, people sang and danced to folk songs in the open air to celebrate the passing of the winter solstice

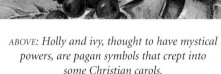

ABOVE: Holly and ivy, thought to have mystical powers, are pagan symbols that crept into some Christian carols.

and the rebirth of spring. But once Christianity spread to Europe, such celebrations came to be regarded with suspicion by religious leaders, largely because of their pagan roots – so much so that the singing (and dancing) of carol songs was banned in some places.

Over the next few centuries, however, the Church had a gradual change of heart, mainly because its clergy could see how enduring the old pagan festivals were among the common people. Church leaders agreed to absorb some of these festivals into the Christian calendar and this may be partly why some of our oldest surviving carols contain a curious mixture of pagan and Christian imagery. Nowhere is this more clearly seen than in *The Holly And The Ivy*, first published in 1710, which includes 'the rising of the sun' in its refrain and may hark back to the midwinter solstice and pre-Christian sun worship.

ABOVE: Despite Church disapproval, carol singing was a popular winter pastime in the medieval period, often with basic musical accompaniment such as a pipe or lute.

EASTER CAROLS

The vast majority of carols that we sing today relate to Christmas – retelling the story of the Nativity and rejoicing at Christ's birth – so they're naturally used to celebrate the festive season. But in medieval times, when the Christian Church took over various pagan traditions, carols were sung as much in celebration of Easter as of Christmas. Among the early Eastertide examples is *The Waits Carol*, probably originating in the 16th century and most likely sung during Lent as it retells the story of Christ dying on the Cross. One Victorian who did much to revive the tradition of carol singing at Easter as well as Christmas was J.M. Neale, an Anglican clergyman. Neale published various books of carols for Christmas and Easter, including a free translation of the 14th-century German carol *In Dulci Jubilo*, 'Good Christian Men, Rejoice'. This carol also looks ahead to Easter and Christ's eventual role as Redeemer of mankind.

RIGHT: This carving of the Virgin and Child standing on a 'Green Man' figure in Exeter Cathedral, Devon, symbolizes the blend of Christian and pagan imagery found in our oldest carols.

ABOVE: *This Edwardian Easter greetings card celebrates spring and Jesus' role as the 'Lamb of God'.*

The cult of the crib

Many of our favourite Christmas carols owe their origin to the ancient practice – more than 900 years old – of placing a crib in church during the Christmas period, with figurines representing the characters in the Nativity story. Although St Francis of Assisi, the founder of the Franciscan Order, is credited with introducing 'the cult of the crib' at Grecchio in Italy in the 13th century, there is evidence of singing and dancing around cribs in other Italian churches even earlier than this.

This shift in focus to Jesus' birth was a fertile source of narrative for later carol composers and gave us the romanticized versions of the Nativity contained in some of the best-loved carols: *Silent Night*; *God Rest You Merry, Gentlemen*; and *Unto Us A Boy Is Born*.

The Franciscans are credited with bringing the first true Christmas carols to the United Kingdom in the 14th century, along with their Christian message. Their 'repertoire' included the earliest known English example, *A Child Is Boren Amonges Man*, reportedly found in a Franciscan friar's sermon notes from around the same period. This ancient carol is still popular today, especially with world-leading choirs such as that at King's College, Cambridge.

ABOVE: A stained-glass window in Canterbury Cathedral depicts the traditional Nativity story so beloved of carol composers.

Storytelling

Music scholars generally agree that the period from 1400 to 1550 was the heyday of the English carol, by now firmly established as a popular form of religious song. Among the carols surviving from this time, and still popular today, are *Adam Lay Y'Bounden*, *A Child This Day Is Born* and *On Christmas Night All Christians Sing*.

Carols increasingly now focused on the simple storytelling of Christ's birth, rather than generally praising God, with the pastoral element of the Nativity – represented by the lowly shepherds – echoed much later in far grander musical works such as Handel's *Messiah* (the 'Shepherd's Chorus'), composed in 1741.

Many Christmas and Easter songs were composed for the open-air mystery plays that were popular in medieval times; the best known of these is the 'Coventry Carol', so called because it was first performed in the city during the Pageant of the Shearmen and the Tailors between 1400 and 1450.

ABOVE: An 18th-century portrait of Handel with the score of the Messiah. *The 'Shepherd's Chorus' echoes the pastoral element found in many Christmas carols.*

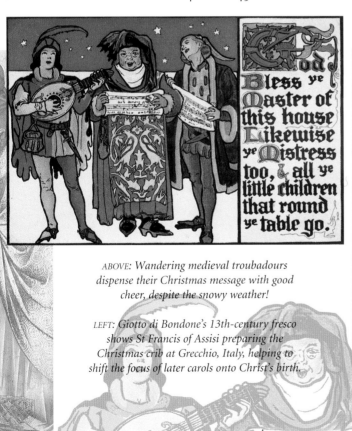

God Bless ye Master of this house Likewise ye Mistress too, & all ye little children that round ye table go.

ABOVE: Wandering medieval troubadours dispense their Christmas message with good cheer, despite the snowy weather!

LEFT: Giotto di Bondone's 13th-century fresco shows St Francis of Assisi preparing the Christmas crib at Grecchio, Italy, helping to shift the focus of later carols onto Christ's birth.

WHEN IS A CAROL NOT A CAROL?

The true English carol – that composed in medieval times – can be distinguished by having a refrain or 'burden', usually a rhyming couplet repeated after each verse. This harks back to the carol's roots in folk songs. True carols also have down-to-earth narratives written in the vernacular while hymns often contain more complex theological ideas and teachings, accompanied by a stricter musical framework. *The Oxford Companion to Music* suggests that carols are distinguished by their 'simplicity of thought and diction, of sincerity and of rhyming brightness'. That said, many of the carols we sing today – for example, *While Shepherds Watched Their Flocks By Night* – started out as scriptural paraphrases.

The Twelve Days Of Christmas

The source of the song *The Twelve Days Of Christmas* – and its text – has long been the subject of debate among music scholars. It is thought to have been written in the late 16th century, a time when Catholic worship was illegal in England and anyone caught practising the faith could be imprisoned or, worse still, executed.

The (unproven) theory is that *The Twelve Days Of Christmas* was composed by Catholics as a way of passing on the basics of their faith in secular code to escape detection, and certain punishment, by Protestant leaders. Each line of the song's rhyme is supposed to represent a different Catholic belief – though much of the symbolism is relevant to Protestants too– and the 'true love' referred to in the first line of the song may be God. Meanwhile, the 'me' may refer to everyone who has been baptized, for it is they who will receive God's gifts in Heaven.

It has been suggested that the song is actually based on a traditional game of forfeits that was accompanied by gift-giving and used to be played on Twelfth Night. But, for most of us, the mysterious 'Catholic code' is still a much more intriguing interpretation of this old favourite!

ABOVE: *The song* The Twelve Days Of Christmas *may have accompanied the game of forfeits traditionally played on Twelfth Night, which included gift-giving – hence the lady's telltale bulging pinafore in this Victorian family scene.*

A partridge in a pear tree
The partridge is said to represent Jesus Christ – mother partridges pretend they are injured to decoy predators from their young and this could parallel Christ's sacrifice on the Cross.

Two turtle doves
The Bible's Old and New Testaments.

Three French hens
Faith, hope and charity.

ABOVE: The geese laying six eggs, depicted here on a kilim rug, may have been a symbol for God's creation of the world in six days.

LEFT: One theory suggests that the partridge in a pear tree represents Jesus Christ and is one of many secret symbols in this catechism song for young Catholics in the 17th century.

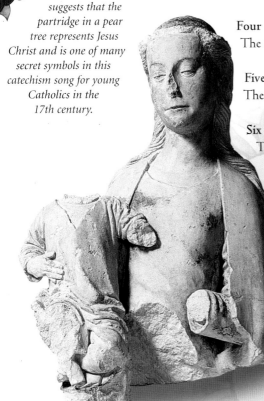

ABOVE: This statue of the Madonna and Child in Winchester Cathedral was considered 'papist' and consequently damaged after the Dissolution of the Monasteries.

Four calling birds
The four Gospels: Matthew, Mark, Luke and John.

Five gold rings
The first five books of the Old Testament.

Six geese a-laying
The six days in which God created the world.

Seven swans a-swimming
The seven sacraments of the Catholic faith.

Eight maids a-milking
The eight Beatitudes.

Nine ladies dancing
The nine fruits of the Holy Spirit.

Ten lords a-leaping
The Ten Commandments.

Eleven pipers piping
Jesus' eleven faithful disciples.

Twelve drummers drumming
The twelve points of belief in the Apostles' Creed.

The Puritans

The Reformation in the 16th and early 17th century, and the Puritan movement that followed, severely curbed the practice of carol singing in church, with the prevailing view – first promoted by Jean Calvin, leader of the Swiss Reformation, and taken up by Protestants in Britain – that only metrical psalms could be heard in God's house.

In Germany, however, the Protestant leader Martin Luther enjoyed and encouraged congregational singing and this had the opposite effect, with various 'folk-style' carols being written and put to well-known tunes, enhancing their general popularity even further. Luther may even have accompanied his family on the lute when they went out carol singing at Christmas time.

ABOVE: In this Victorian painting, 17th-century carol singers receive the wassail bowl as reward for their efforts.

ABOVE: Night watchmen, or 'waits', originally called the hours, but this childlike depiction of them looks forward to their later role as house-to-house carol singers.

A Very Happy Christmas

· THE · WAITS ·
WE COME ASINGING TO YOUR GATES,
SO LISTEN AT YOUR LEISURE!
WE ARE THE MERRY CHRISTMAS WAITS,
WHO WISH YOU PEACE & PLEASURE!

A wassailing we will go

One of the main reasons that carols remained so popular 'on the streets', despite the Puritans' hatred of this 'pagan' activity, was the fact that such songs remained part of family celebrations at Christmas. Carols continued to be sung in the open air and wherever people gathered socially, in the taverns, village halls and meeting houses across England.

'Waits', or night watchmen, had traditionally announced the night-time hours around the towns and cities for centuries and wassailing, an old West Country tradition, involved singing around the orchards on Twelfth Night to scare away evil spirits. These two traditions joined forces to create house-to-house carol singing, which became an integral part of the Christmas experience into the 19th and 20th centuries, although the practice is rather more patchily observed today.

RAISING A GLASS ...

The traditional English carol *Here We Come A Wassailing* is full of the merriment associated with the adventures of carol singing around the houses, as well as the alcohol consumed by the carollers at each stop! So goes the carol: 'Our wassail cup is made of the rosemary tree and so is your beer of the best barley.' The wassail brew was a potent mix of ale, cider and/or wine, citrus, sugar and spices.

ABOVE: Cranach the Elder's 16th-century portrait of Reformation leader Martin Luther, who helped popularize carol singing in Europe.

THE DAY CHRISTMAS CAROLS WERE BANNED

In 1644, the parliamentary leader and zealous Puritan Oliver Cromwell persuaded his Long Parliament to ban Christmas celebrations. As though to drive home their disapproval of anything and everything to do with this festive season, the Puritans also held parliamentary sessions on 25 December every year up to 1656. It wasn't until the Restoration of the 'merry monarch' Charles II in 1660 that the ban on Christmas celebrations was lifted.

Even then the Church retained strict control over what could and couldn't be sung during services, and the only officially approved Christmas carol was *While Shepherds Watched Their Flocks By Night* because it paraphrased St Luke's biblical account of the Nativity. In 1700, this carol gained itself the ultimate religious acceptance – being bound into a supplement of *The New Version of the Psalms* – but it took another 80 years or so before *Hark! The Herald Angels Sing* and four other carols were added.

LEFT: Carol singing remained popular in the home despite the Puritans' ban of all things 'Christmas' in the mid 17th century.

RIGHT: This exceptionally ornate 17th-century wassail bowl, in mother-of-pearl mounted on silver, is on display in the Victoria and Albert Museum, London.

What the Victorians did for carols

The Victorians were enthusiastic revivalists and enjoyed reinventing various English traditions, including Christmas – and the Christmas carol along with it. The Church of England, Methodists and Baptists all wanted to encourage more people to attend their church services, and carol singing was so popular among the general public that Church leaders recognized its appeal.

By bringing carols in from the open air where they'd been sung since medieval times by wandering musicians, waits and wassailers, carols now started to attract people into church in much greater numbers, especially at Christmas and Easter time. The High Church or 'Oxford' Movement of the early and mid 19th century played a significant role in this new trend by introducing hymns and carols into the liturgy.

Three Victorians who particularly helped carols gain greater acceptance in the Church were J.M. Neale, who edited the 1853 *Carols For Christmas-tide*, including Continental carols as well as his own contribution *Good King Wenceslas*, and the 1871 collaboration between H.R. Bramley and J. Stainer, *Carols Old And New*, making carols more accessible to clergy and organists alike.

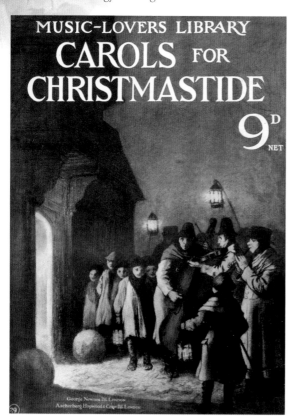

LEFT: *A burst of publishing activity in the 19th and 20th centuries, including this 9d* Carols for Christmastide, *helped preserve some of our oldest carols and brought them to a wider audience.*

LEFT: This Victorian Christmas card shows children singing carols underneath the lighted tree, another Victorian 'tradition'.

A CHRISTMAS CAROL

Charles Dickens' most famous work, *A Christmas Carol*, written in 1834, showed its Victorian readers that Christmas could be celebrated as a cosy, one-day event at home with the family, rather than the traditional 12-day Yuletide feast attended by whole villages or communities. And Christmas carols still had their part to play in the celebrations, as they did in the telling of Dickens' story.

ABOVE: In this charming 18th-century painting, the village choirmaster leads his merry band in their carol singing while members of the household listen at the door.

RIGHT: This Victorian scene of cosy domesticity sums up the sentiment of Charles Dickens' novel A Christmas Carol, *which firmly placed the festivities in the family home.*

The Methodists

In Britain, the carol and hymn stock was greatly boosted in the 1700s by the compositions of Charles Wesley, brother of Methodist founder John Wesley. Charles wrote more than 6,000 hymn texts in his lifetime and a number of these, including some carols, were revived by the Victorians. For example, *Hark! The Herald Angels Sing* is a Wesley composition, though the words are much changed from his original *Hark, How All The Welkin Rings* written in the mid 1700s.

Many of the carols that we now think of as being traditional 'old English' were actually written in North America in the 19th century. They include *O Little Town Of Bethlehem*, *It Came Upon The Midnight Clear* and *We Three Kings*. And the first written record of that most famous of children's carols *Away In A Manger* was in Philadelphia in 1885.

ABOVE: *Commemorated in this stained-glass window in Wesley's Chapel, London, the Wesley Brothers were founding Methodists and Charles was responsible for composing many of the 'standards' in today's hymn and carol books.*

MORALS ...

The Victorians were keen to encourage good morals among the general population and this was carried through into the text of many carols written around this time. Hence, in Edward Caswell's *See Amid The Winter's Snow*, first printed in 1851, the plea goes out: 'Teach, O teach us, holy child, by thy face so meek and mild, Teach us to resemble thee in thy sweet humility.' And in *Once In Royal David's City*, first published in 1848, Christian children are reminded '... all must be, mild, obedient, good as He'.

BELOW: This painting from around 1860 shows the village church brimming with parishioners keen to practise their carol singing under the watchful eye of the vicar.

ABOVE: Church carol services have long been a popular way of attracting large congregations, as shown in this romantic snowy scene.

... AND MUSIC

Many Victorian 'revival' carols started out simply as texts that were then fitted to well-known folk music, making them easy to learn and instantly familiar to the general public. A good example of this is *While Shepherds Watched Their Flocks By Night*, originally a hymn, which has been set to a range of tunes, including the melody that is now more commonly associated with the folk song *On Ilkley Moor Baht'at*. Several carols also had different tunes in North America – for example, *Away In A Manger* is sung to a tune with which we are not generally familiar in the United Kingdom.

Carol services

Church services designed specifically around carol singing only really became popular in late Victorian times; by then, carols had firmly re-established themselves as popular religious songs, though they'd never gone 'out of fashion' among rural communities.

Festival of carols

Church carol singing was greatly boosted by the example of the 'Festival of Nine Lessons and Carols' created by Church leaders in Cornwall, which quickly caught on in other areas.

We have the Reverend G.H.S. Walpole and Bishop E.W. Benson to thank for this 'new' form of church service, which was first used on Christmas Eve in 1880 at Truro Cathedral, then no more than a wooden hut. The cathedral's choir had, two years earlier, decided to switch their usual Christmas Eve tradition of singing around the city in favour of a service of lessons, carols and a sermon held in the cathedral at 10pm.

The 'festival' built on that change by organizing the service into a formulaic setting of nine lessons, nine carols and, of course, the Christmas sermon. Benson's son later recalled: 'My father arranged from ancient sources, a little service for Christmas Eve – nine carols and nine tiny lessons, which were read by various officers of the Church, beginning with a chorister and ending … with the Bishop.'

Ever since then, the 'Festival of Nine Lessons and Carols' has become a popular model for Christmas carol services throughout the United Kingdom and the wider Christian world from the West Indies to the Far East.

ABOVE: An early 16th-century window depicting the Queen of Sheba visiting Solomon, in King's College Chapel, Cambridge.

LEFT: Candlelight adds that special something to a Christmas carol service at 800-year-old St David's Cathedral in Pembrokeshire.

ABOVE: King's College Chapel in Cambridge has hosted the 'Festival of Nine Lessons and Carols' for more than 80 years, broadcast across the world annually since 1928.

Carols at King's

Perhaps the most famous carol service still using this framework today is the 'Festival of Nine Lessons and Carols' that has been held on Christmas Eve at King's College Chapel in Cambridge every year since 1918. The service was first broadcast on radio by the BBC in 1928 and has been so annually except in 1930, even continuing throughout the Second World War when the ancient Chapel's precious stained-glass windows (and any heat!) had been removed for protection.

At King's, the service, lessons and prayers remain unchanged from year to year but different carols are chosen. A chorister always reads the first lesson, harking back to that first carol service in Truro, and many people would agree that Christmas hasn't 'started' until they hear those crystal-clear opening lines sung by a solo boy chorister: 'Once in royal David's city stood a lowly cattle shed …'.

THE CHILDREN'S CHRISTINGLE

Traditionally held on the Sunday before Christmas, this children's service from the Moravian Church in Germany has steadily gained popularity in the United Kingdom over the last 40 years, with children's carols such as *Away In A Manger* and *Little Donkey* being popular choices.

The Moravian Church first held its Christingle service on 24 December 1747 as part of the Marienborn Congregation's wider Christmas Children's Festival. But it wasn't until 1968 that the Christingle was introduced to the Church of England by The Children's Society, as a way of celebrating 'the family'. Churches across the UK now hold their own versions of this much-loved family event.

The service includes popular carols, lessons and prayers read by children and, at the climax, each child is given a lighted candle that represents Christ, the light of the world. The Moravian carol 'Morning Star, O Cheering Sight' is traditionally sung when each child receives their candle and the church lights are dimmed to let Christ's light – the candles – shine through the gloom.

ABOVE: Today, children's carol services often feature the 'Christingle', an orange with a lighted candle that represents the world and Christ, the light of the world.

Some of the oldest

On Christmas Night All Christians Sing

Also known as 'The Sussex Carol' because this is where two
20th-century folk-song revivalists collected it. *On Christmas
Night* was first published in a small volume of carols by Irish
bishop Luke Wadding in 1684 at Ghent in the Low Countries.
But its tune is that composed by Mrs Verrall and arranged for
choral singing along with seven other traditional carols by the
composer Ralph Vaughan Williams in 1920.

Unto Us A Boy Is Born

Editor of the influential collection *Songs of Praise*, north
London vicar Percy Dearmer translated this carol from
what he termed a 'rollicking' 15th-century Latin text for
The Oxford Book of Carols, first published in 1928.

*ABOVE: A window in York Minster shows Adam
about to eat the apple in the Garden of Eden, the
focus for one of our oldest surviving carol texts,
Adam Lay Y'Bounden.*

Adam Lay Y'Bounden

The original music to the text of this 15th-century carol
has not survived, so 20th-century composers have set it to
various tunes. It is a rare form of carol because it makes
no reference to Jesus or the Nativity, focusing instead on
Adam's original sin, eating the apple in the Garden of Eden.
And typical of other medieval carols, it mixes Latin phrases
with the vernacular text, with its refrain 'Deo Gracias!'

Telling the Story

ABOVE LEFT: *The score and lyrics for* Stille Nacht, Heilige Nacht, *written in an Alpine village at Christmas in the early 19th century.*

LEFT: *The subject matter for the majority of carols sung today is that most endearing of narratives, the birth of Jesus Christ.*

Silent Night, Holy Night

Originally *Stille Nacht, Heilige Nacht*, this carol is so popular that it even has its own website (www.silentnight.com). The story goes that it was composed in haste by the local priest and his organist at Christmas in 1818 after a mouse ate through the organ wires in St Nicholas' Church in Oberndorf, Austria. While the story has been somewhat romanticized, it is true that the two men worked together on it and *Stille Nacht* was first performed by two male voices accompanied by guitar at that very church in Oberndorf.

While Shepherds Watched Their Flocks By Night

Penned by the 6th Poet Laureate of England, Nahum Tate, this carol is a universal favourite with adults and children alike, although it has also suffered many parodies, the most infamous being 'While shepherds washed their socks by night'! Nahum Tate sadly died in a debtors' prison but his enduring hymn was the first Christmas carol officially allowed in church services, being added to a *Supplement to the New Version of the Psalms* in 1700.

God Rest You Merry, Gentlemen

Experts believe this carol has been sung in London for at least 300 years and, today, it is still sung to the 'London' tune. Its first line 'God rest you merry, gentlemen' means 'God keep you merry', and much has been made of the 'lost comma' after the word 'merry' in the first line! The carol may date back to an age when the lord of the manor would invite local peasants to share in his Christmas festivities. One can imagine the poor people greeting their lord at table with this jolly but comforting carol in which we are reminded that Jesus himself was born a peasant, lying in a manger.

Rejoicing!

Hark! The Herald Angels Sing

Hark! The Herald Angels Sing derives from a hymn for
Christmas Day written by the great Methodist hymn-writer
Charles Wesley in 1739. The original began 'Hark, how all
the welkin [sky] rings' and it was altered by several hands to
make the carol we know today; the familiar tune to which it
is now sung was actually written as a cantata by the German
composer Mendelssohn, to celebrate the 400th anniversary
of the invention of printing.

Ding, Dong, Merrily On High!

This relatively modern carol (it was written in the early
20th century) is based on an old French dance song, harking
back to the original meaning of 'carol' as a secular dance
tune. It is the work of the Reverend George Woodward, who
published several important carol anthologies around the
turn of the last century, and includes a Latin refrain 'Gloria,
Hosanna in Excelsis!' as did earlier medieval carols.

ABOVE: Good King Wenceslas' *concern for 'yonder
peasant' provided just the sort of charitable tale
needed for Boxing Day, when churches traditionally
gave alms to the poor.*

*References to a snowy setting for the
Nativity crept into some carols from
the 19th century onwards.*

A White Christmas

In The Bleak Midwinter
Dante Gabriel Rossetti's sister Christina, a poet, hymnwriter and Anglican, wrote this as a poem but it became a hymn after it was published in *The English Hymnal* in 1906. A generous slice of poetic licence allowed Christina to set the Nativity in a wintry setting and Gustav Holst's memorable tune secured this carol's future popularity.

Good King Wenceslas
This Boxing Day carol came fourth in a 1996 Gallup poll of the most popular Christmas carols and was written by J.M. Neale in the 1850s to fit an old Scandinavian folk-carol tune used during springtime. Boxing Day is St Stephen's Day, traditionally when charitable works were undertaken, hence the term 'boxing', thought to refer to the alms boxes distributed to the poor on this day. Good King Wenceslas echoes this spirit of charity, trudging through the winter snow to bring firewood and a meal to a poor peasant.

Children's Carols

Little Donkey
Written by Sunderland schoolteacher Eric Boswell in the 1950s, this carol is unusual in placing a donkey, usually associated with Palm Sunday, in a central role during the Nativity. But it became an instant success upon publication and infant and primary schools across the country still warm to its simple, childlike sentiments and tune.

Away In A Manger
Once thought to be the work of German Protestant leader Martin Luther, this carol actually first appeared in collections of songs for children in America in the 1880s under the title *Luther's Cradle Hymn*, hence the original theory.

BELOW: Since Victorian times, carols have provided a rich source of subject matter for countless Christmas cards.

Collecting carols

It wasn't until the invention of the printing press in the early 16th century that music printing became available. Because of their popularity, carols were printed and distributed widely, often on single sheets of paper called 'broadsides'. These were sold for a penny on the streets of most large cities, especially London, and made singing together in groups a much easier proposition for the general public. While most people did not buy or collect books in the same way as today, it meant that the words and music to many of our oldest carols survived.

A great burst of publishing activity that started in the early 19th century and continued right through Victorian times into the 20th century gave us various collections of traditional hymns and carols, also helping to preserve them for future generations. Among the most significant are Sir Humphry Davys' *Collection of Christmas Carols*, published in 1822, *Carols for Christmas-tide* (1853) and *Carols for Easter-tide* (1854), edited by the Reverends J.M. Neale and T. Helmore, and the Reverend H.R. Bramley's collection of 42 carols called *Christmas Carols New And Old* (1871).

RIGHT: Once printing became widespread, many carols were printed onto 'broadsides', penny music sheets that were hawked on the streets as shown in this 19th-century painting by A.E. Mulready.

MODERN-DAY CAROLS

John Rutter is perhaps the most famous of our modern composers to turn his hand to carols, writing the words and music to the joyous and ever popular *Shepherd's Pipe Carol* in 1966 while studying at Clare College, Cambridge. Rutter wanted the accompanying music to mimic 'bright woodwind piping' and it has quickly achieved the 'classic' status normally reserved for some of our older carols. Other successful modern carol writers include John Bell, and Graham Kendrick who has written various Christmas songs, including one composed specifically for The Children's Society's annual Christingle service in 1997.

The folk revival

Into the 20th century, there was a surge in interest in old folk songs after the formation of the Folk-Song Society in 1898. This fuelled various collections of old carols that might otherwise have been lost, with Cecil Sharp at the forefront of this 'revival', publishing the *English Folk Carols* in 1911.

Today, the origins of our traditional carols are well documented by detailed collections including Professor Dr. Ian Bradley's authoritative guide *The Penguin Book of Carols* and Percy Dearmer's earlier *Oxford Book of Carols*, published in 1928. This had input from the composer Ralph Vaughan Williams, himself an avid collector of genuine old folk-carol tunes.

Thanks to such work, the interest in carol singing rekindled by the Victorians was consolidated in the 20th century and has secured the carol's important role in today's – and our future – celebration of Christ's birth.